SO YOU WANT TO BE A

NINJA?

Written by
BRUNO VINCENT

Illustrated by
TAKAYO AKIYAMA

Inspired by the book by
STEPHEN TURNBULL

Thames & Hudson

First published in 2020 in the United States of America by
Thames & Hudson Inc., 500 Fifth Avenue, New York, New York 10110

www.thamesandhudsonusa.com

Library of Congress Control Number 2019957436

ISBN 978-0-500-65210-7

Printed and bound in China by Everbest Printing Co. Ltd

SO YOU WANT TO BE A NINJA?

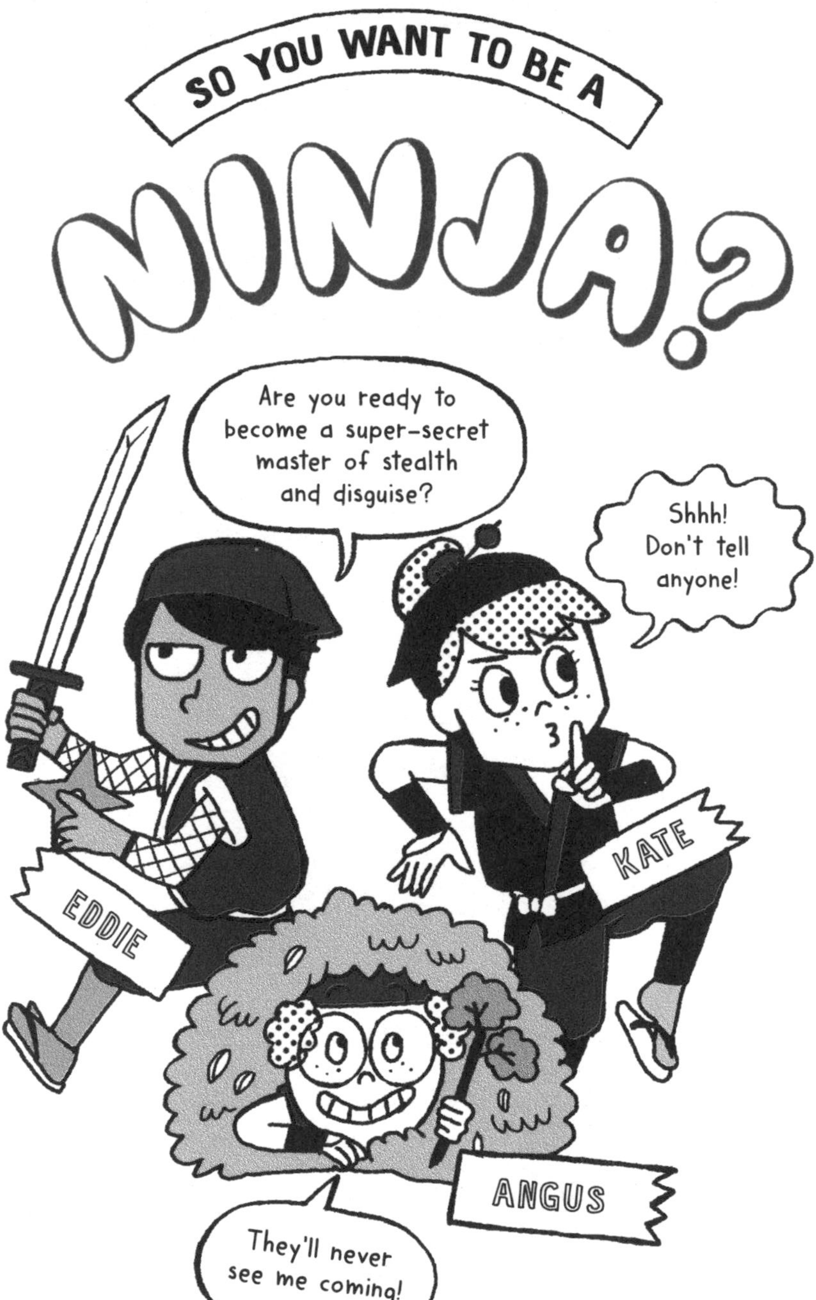
Are you ready to become a super-secret master of stealth and disguise?
EDDIE
Shhh! Don't tell anyone!
KATE
ANGUS
They'll never see me coming!

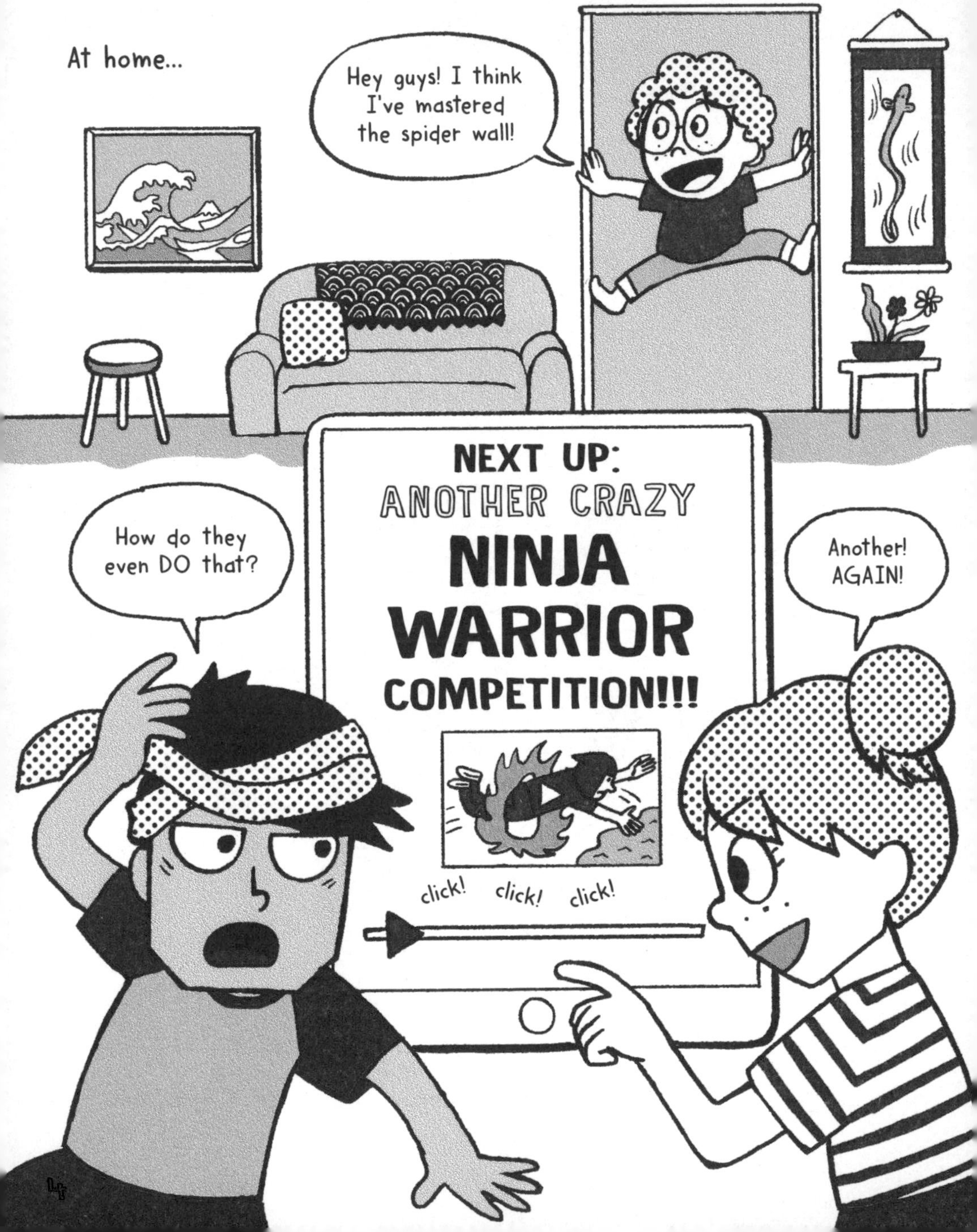
At home...
Hey guys! I think I've mastered the spider wall!
How do they even DO that?
NEXT UP: ANOTHER CRAZY NINJA WARRIOR COMPETITION!!!
Another! AGAIN!
click! click! click!

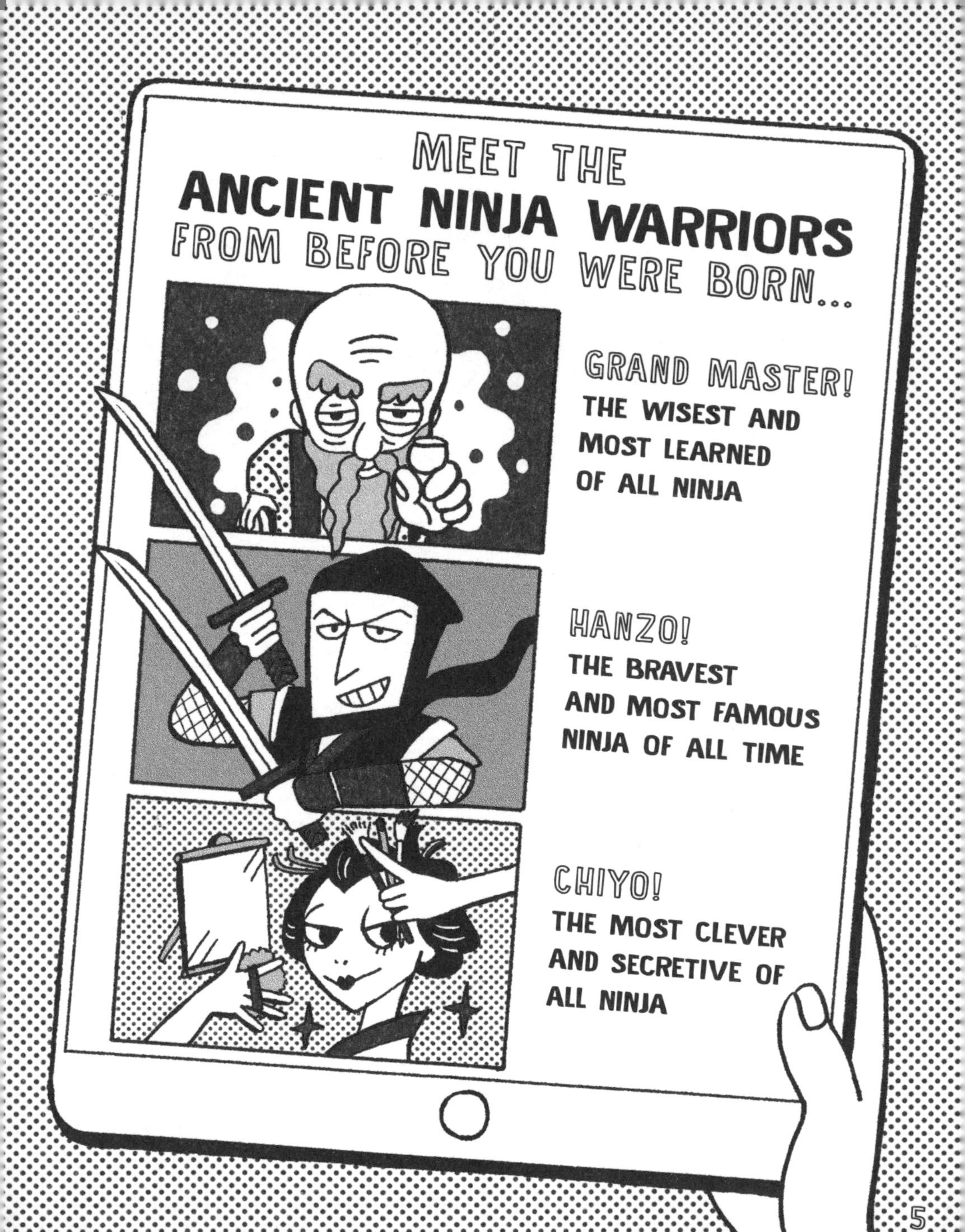
MEET THE
ANCIENT NINJA WARRIORS
FROM BEFORE YOU WERE BORN...
GRAND MASTER!
THE WISEST AND MOST LEARNED OF ALL NINJA
HANZO!
THE BRAVEST AND MOST FAMOUS NINJA OF ALL TIME
CHIYO!
THE MOST CLEVER AND SECRETIVE OF ALL NINJA

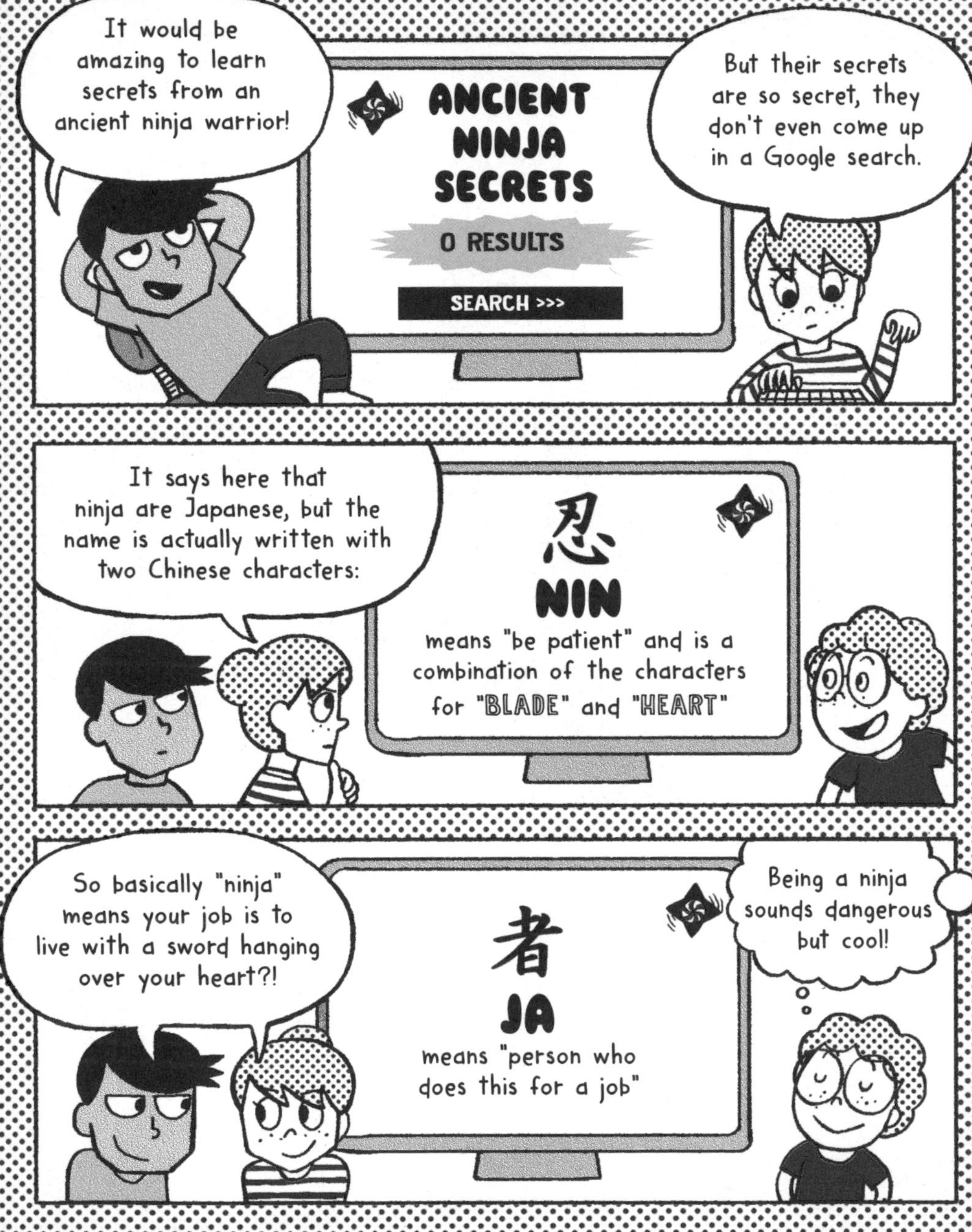
It would be amazing to learn secrets from an ancient ninja warrior!
ANCIENT NINJA SECRETS
0 RESULTS
SEARCH >>>
But their secrets are so secret, they don't even come up in a Google search.
It says here that ninja are Japanese, but the name is actually written with two Chinese characters:
忍
NIN
means "be patient" and is a combination of the characters for "BLADE" and "HEART"
So basically "ninja" means your job is to live with a sword hanging over your heart?!
者
JA
means "person who does this for a job"
Being a ninja sounds dangerous but cool!

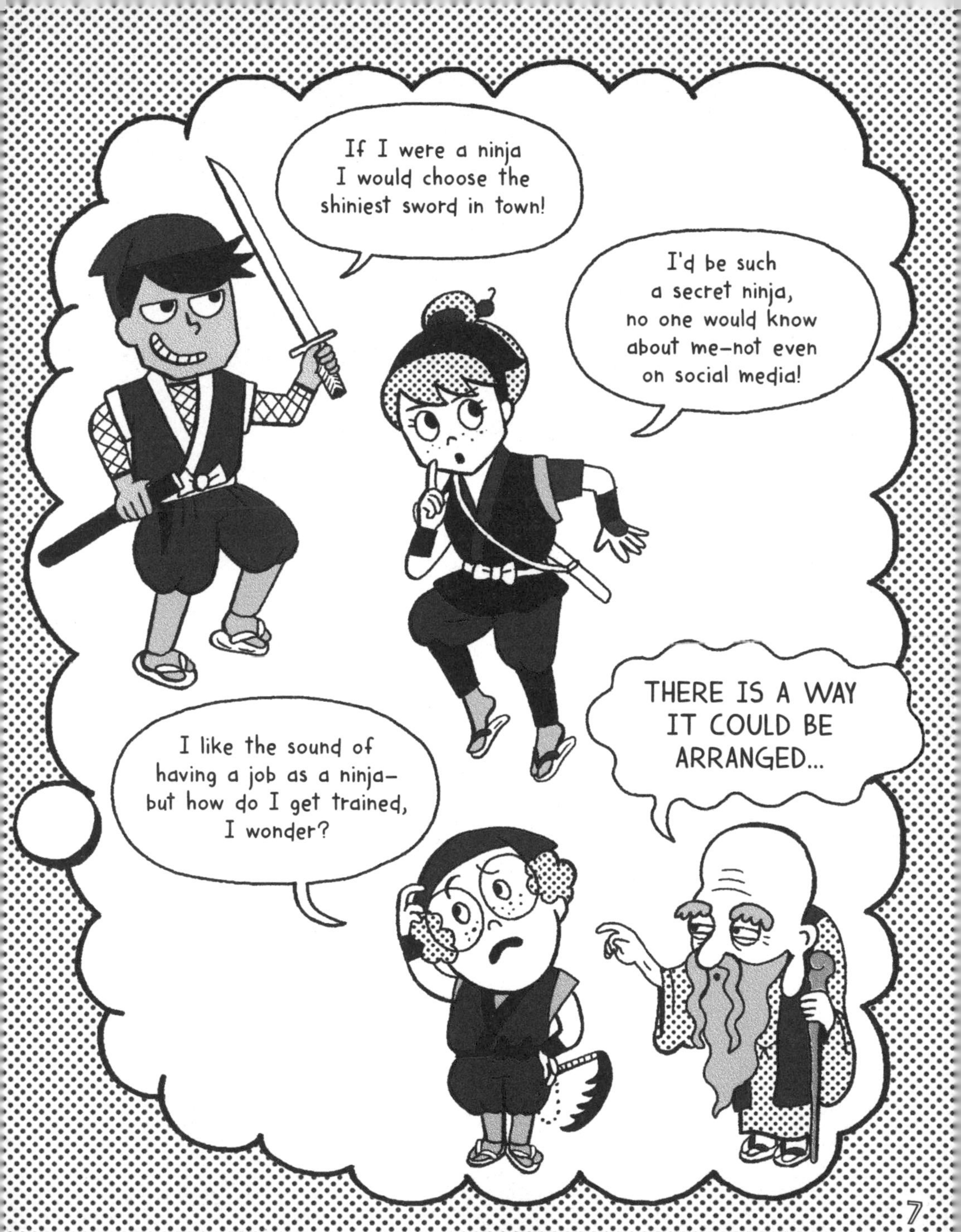
If I were a ninja I would choose the shiniest sword in town!
I'd be such a secret ninja, no one would know about me—not even on social media!
I like the sound of having a job as a ninja—but how do I get trained, I wonder?
THERE IS A WAY IT COULD BE ARRANGED...

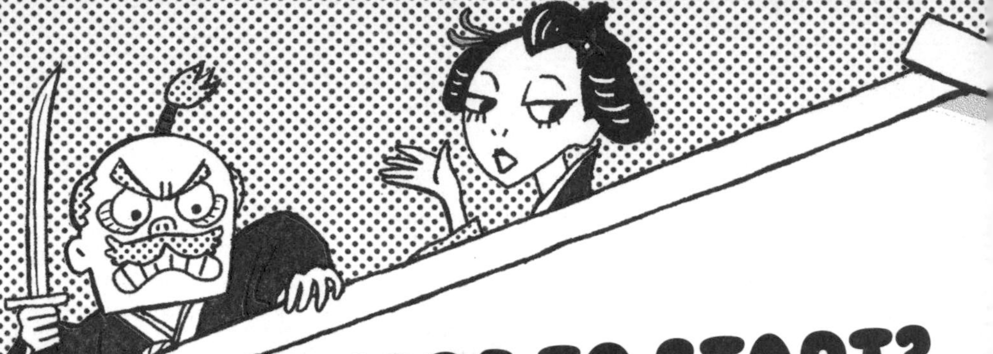

WHERE TO START?

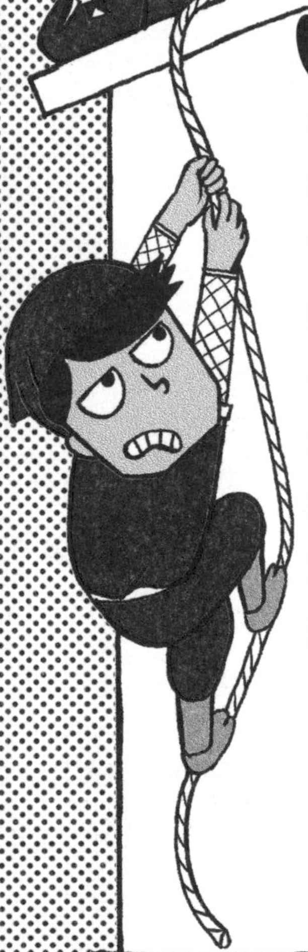

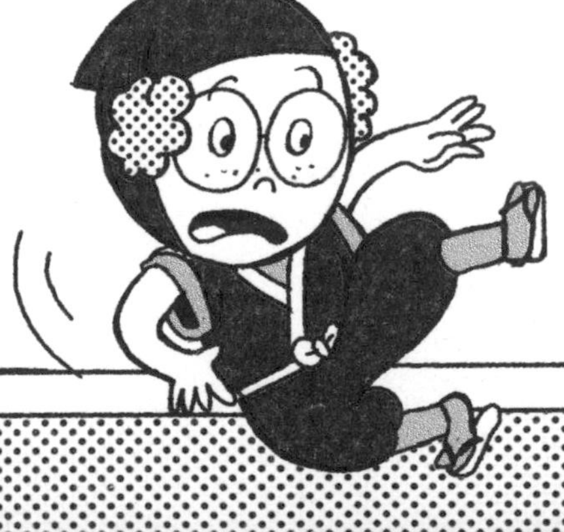

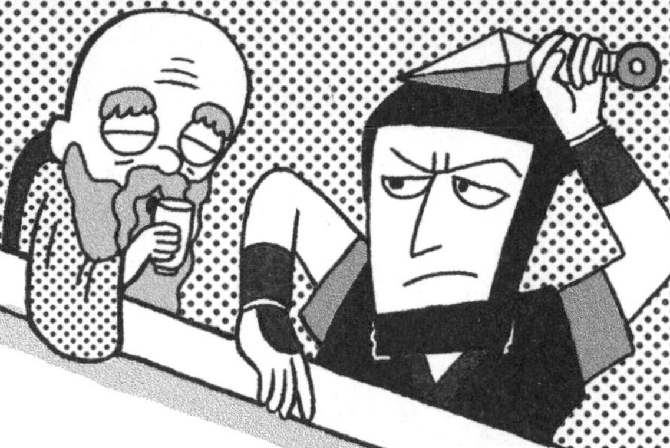

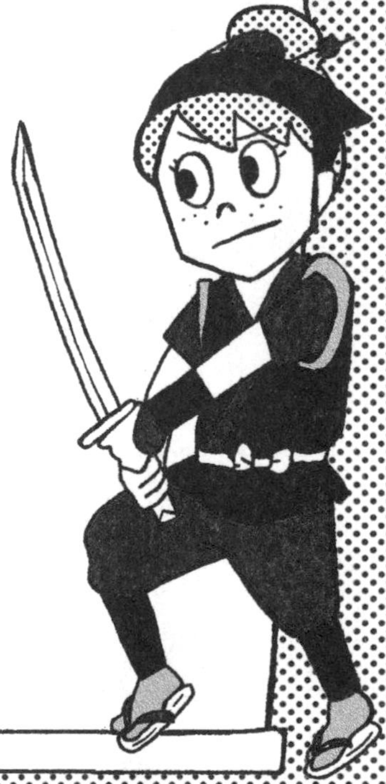

SO YOU WANT TO BE A ... NINJA?

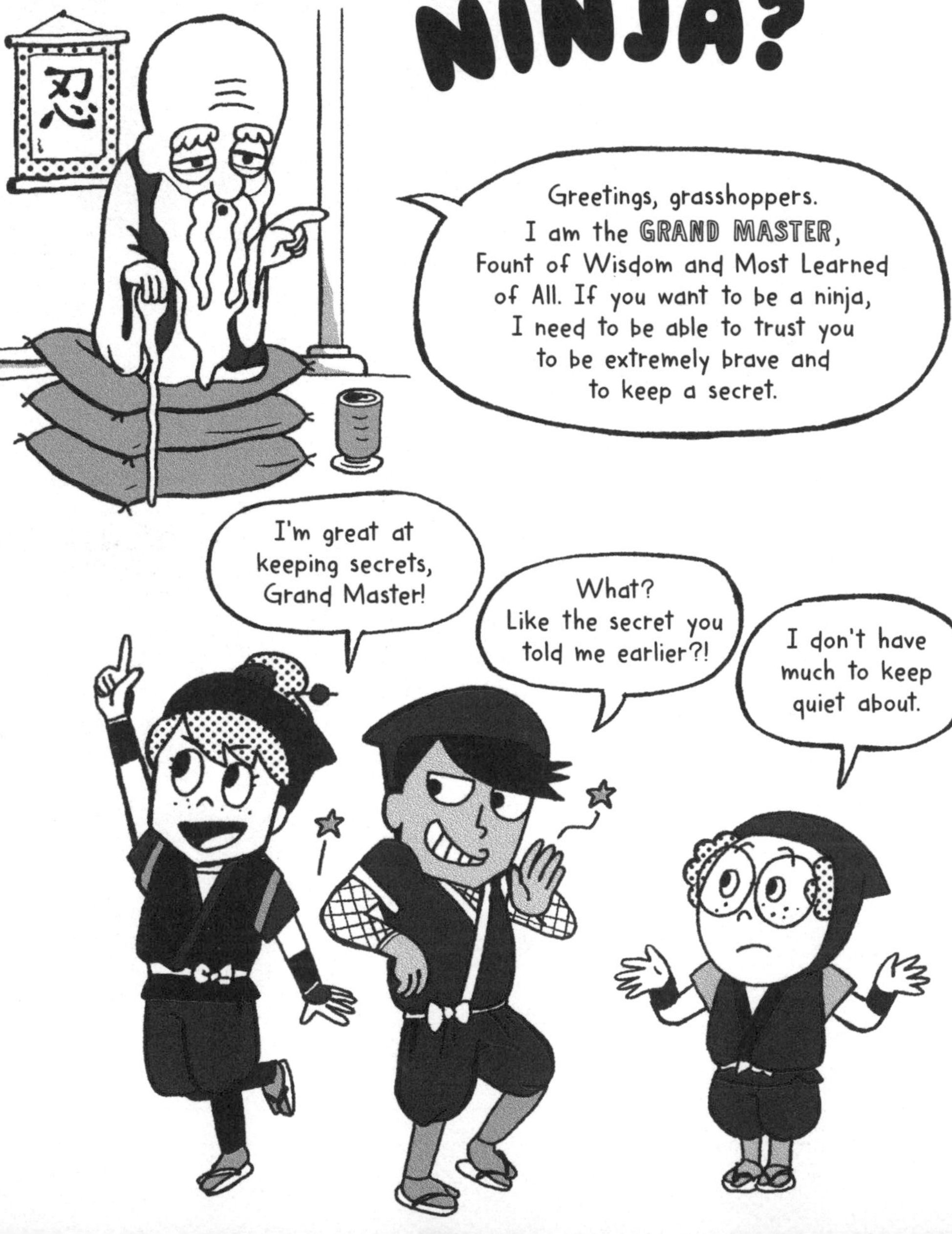

忍
Greetings, grasshoppers. I am the GRAND MASTER, Fount of Wisdom and Most Learned of All. If you want to be a ninja, I need to be able to trust you to be extremely brave and to keep a secret.
I'm great at keeping secrets, Grand Master!
What? Like the secret you told me earlier?!
I don't have much to keep quiet about.

THE SECRET SCROLL OF THE NINJA

In this SUPER-SECRET scroll you will discover
the secrets to becoming a world-class ninja.
Ninja live to serve His Most Illustrious Highness,
the Shogun of Japan, guarding Edo Castle
and keeping the peace.

As a ninja you will practice
the secret arts called
"NINJUTSU":

★ SPY AND GATHER INFORMATION

★ BREAK INTO ENEMY GROUNDS

★ CAUSE CHAOS FOR THE ENEMY

You can call me **HANZO**. I am a chunin, or middle ninja of great skill and training. I lead the guards at the historic Edo Castle, where I protect the highest lord of all, the Shogun. This checklist will show whether you are among the very few who qualify to begin training as a ninja!

NINJA CHECKLIST

Check all boxes that apply ☑

1. I AM HAPPY TO WORK WITHOUT FAME OR REWARD

Correcting the injustices of the world is enough for you—and seeing that the right thing is done. Even if you become the greatest, bravest, most brilliant ninja of all time, your work will all be kept a secret and no one will know about it except you.

Did you hear about three kids who are training to become ninja?

12

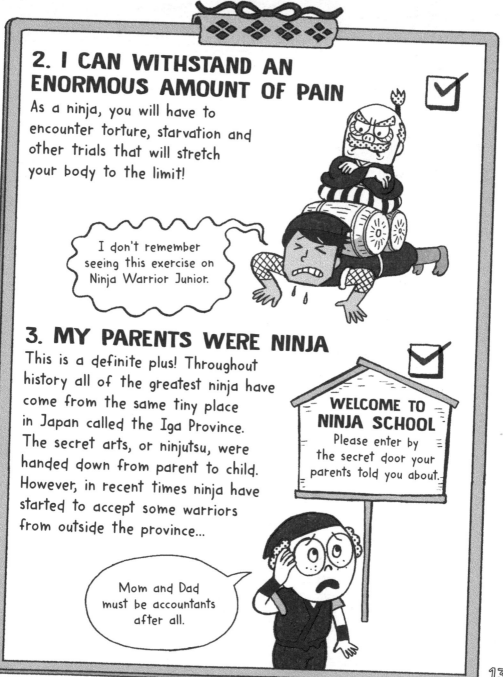

2. I CAN WITHSTAND AN ENORMOUS AMOUNT OF PAIN

As a ninja, you will have to encounter torture, starvation and other trials that will stretch your body to the limit!

> I don't remember seeing this exercise on Ninja Warrior Junior.

3. MY PARENTS WERE NINJA

This is a definite plus! Throughout history all of the greatest ninja have come from the same tiny place in Japan called the Iga Province. The secret arts, or ninjutsu, were handed down from parent to child. However, in recent times ninja have started to accept some warriors from outside the province...

WELCOME TO NINJA SCHOOL
Please enter by the secret door your parents told you about.

> Mom and Dad must be accountants after all.

My name is CHIYO.
I may look like a theater actress, but in fact I am a kunoichi or female ninja with ninja stars in my wig.

4. I AM A WOMAN

Please enter! Girls and women have always been welcomed into the ninja community. Some of the most successful ninja were women and were often more effective and deadly than men thanks to their skill at the art of disguise (see page 28 for more details).

5. I LOOK GOOD IN BLACK

Well, good for you. And, of course, ninja do wear black—when attacking by night. At other hours, however, wearing black is the opposite of useful—it will make you stand out! More important than looking good in black, you must be good at disguising yourself.

Hey! We came in the same disguise!

Parp!

6. I AM A CONVICTED CRIMINAL ☑

Many of our greatest ninja have been criminals. As a convicted criminal you will have useful experience using weapons, breaking into buildings and escaping from the scene of the crime. Plus, you will be happy to disappear from society and lose your identity!

I stole a pencil from Ikea, does that count?

They're free, Kate!

7. I WOULD LOVE TO LIVE IN THE MOUNTAINOUS IGA PROVINCE OF JAPAN ☑

This is good news indeed! The ninja of Iga Province are the greatest of all. It was here long ago that the idea of a band of outlaw spies was refined into the noble art of ninjutsu!

I am the **SHADOW NINJA**, the most mysterious of all your teachers. I am so silent and secretive, you won't even hear me breathe! Take my quiz to see if you truly make the ninja grade...

NINJA QUIZ

1. WHERE DO YOU LIVE?

A — far away from Edo Castle

B — wherever battle takes me

C — by the sea

D — high up in the mountains

2. WHAT'S YOUR FAVORITE FOOD?

A — soba noodles

B — whatever I'm given

C — fresh fish

D — three-year-old cake balls

3. WHAT'S YOUR FAVORITE FASHION ACCESSORY?

A a cloth hat

B a straw hat

C a winged helmet

D a mask

4. WHAT'S YOUR FAVORITE WEAPON?

A a long sword

B a bow and arrow

C a very long sword

D a rope

5. HOW WOULD YOU DESCRIBE YOURSELF?

A hungry for power

B humble and loyal

C greedy for money

D patient but vengeful

COUNT UP YOUR A, B, C AND D ANSWERS. CHECK THE RESULTS ON THE NEXT PAGE >>>

QUIZ RESULTS:

IF YOU CHOSE **MOSTLY A'S** YOU WILL MOST LIKELY BE A:

DAIMYO

Daimyo are warlords who set themselves up as rulers of little patches of land. Daimyo in the Tokugawa Period start to hate and fear their own leader, the Shogun. Many daimyo even want to kill him and take his place! They often fight with one another over small things.

> Hey! That's my puddle!

> Oh no! I've broken my leg and I've still got 100 miles to walk.

MOSTLY B'S

ASHIGARU

In ancient Japan, ashigaru, or foot soldiers, are not as highly respected as they should be. They are sent to fight large battles on foot and can expect to be tricked, spied upon and terrified by the brilliant ways of the ninja!

MOSTLY C'S:

SAMURAI

Compared to ninja, samurai are wealthy, popular, well trained and show-offs. Only the eldest son in a family can become a samurai —how unfair! Ninja HATE them. But the people LOVE them! Samurai are the warriors that ninja most like to take down in battle.

MOSTLY D'S:

NINJA

Ninja warriors prefer secrecy and stealth to the eye-catching methods of other warriors. Plus, unlike the other groups here, they allow women to join. Continue reading this book and begin your training!

WELCOME TO THE NINJA MANSION

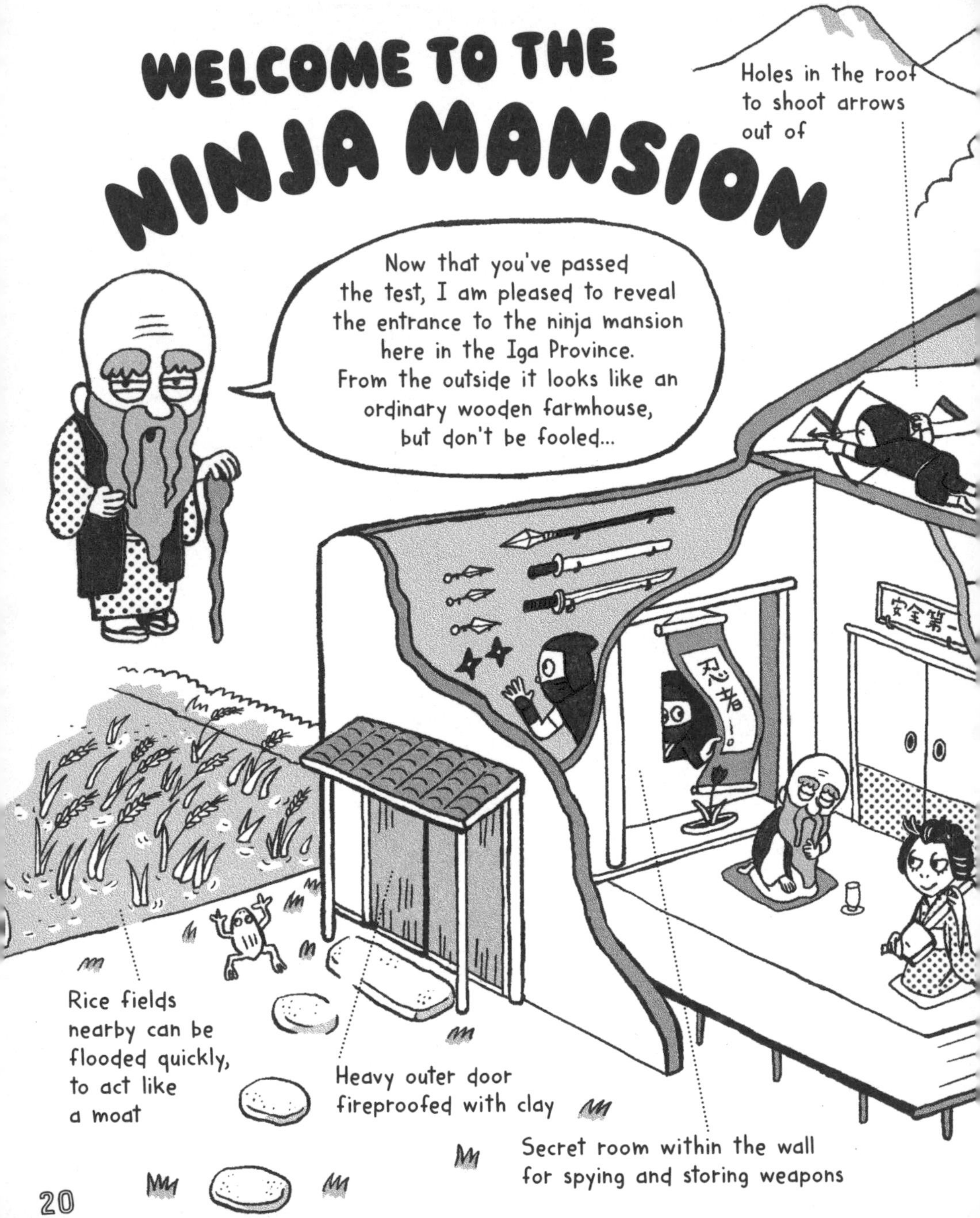

Holes in the roof to shoot arrows out of
Now that you've passed the test, I am pleased to reveal the entrance to the ninja mansion here in the Iga Province. From the outside it looks like an ordinary wooden farmhouse, but don't be fooled...
Rice fields nearby can be flooded quickly, to act like a moat
Heavy outer door fireproofed with clay
Secret room within the wall for spying and storing weapons

Hidden trapdoor to escape out onto the roof via rope ladder

Secret spy holes drilled into the ceiling

Concealed staircase to a hidden room in the roof

Loose floorboards concealing traps

Sliding panels in the wall allow ninja to disappear

21

WELCOME TO NINJA SCHOOL

Now that you've found the door to ninja school, there are some basic skills you need to perfect before things get dangerous.

READING, WRITING AND MATH

Being stealthy means not getting caught, so you'll need to write and read messages that can be followed precisely. Check your spelling and write all numbers the correct way round.

Is that a six or a nine?! If I weren't so stealthy I would scream right now!

Dear Kate,

Take the 9th door— all others lead to danger.

Your ninja brother, Angus. xx

MEGA MEMORY

If you get caught in the middle of a mission, a map can be used as evidence against you. You need to be able to look at a map just once and memorize it exactly.

Ah-ha! At the fork, we take the road that ends in a house...

PERFECT BALANCE

Most castles are protected by high walls and a moat of water. If you can't walk on water or fly, you should learn how to cross a moat by balancing on a narrow stick of bamboo. Although it may look slender, bamboo is incredibly strong.

CAT-LIKE AGILITY

To break into secret locations, you'll need to squeeze through gaps and hang upside-down by your fingertips. Take a lesson from the cat who walks through tiny spaces and climbs rooftops like a pro. (Ancient ninja were known to dislocate their joints to squeeze into very narrow gaps, but this isn't recommended.)

NEXT-LEVEL CALM

Ninja must remain calm and silent in the most challenging situations. They are encouraged to meditate daily and have to learn to breathe without making a sound. To do this, you must achieve a state known as FUDOSHIN or "immoveable heart"– this means your heart rate always stays steady even after a big scare.

ODORLESS AND UNSCENTED

It's vital that a ninja's odor doesn't give them away. Guard dogs will sniff out a ninja with a strong smell, good or bad. So you need to wash regularly and avoid perfumes or smelly food.

✗ don't eat garlic
✗ don't eat onions
✔ stay away from smoke or other strong smells like perfume
✔ wash yourself regularly

HIDE UNDERWATER

Once you have become fit enough to breathe without making a sound, your lungs will be strong enough to breathe through a tube underwater. This will come in handy when you need to hide for hours under the surface of a lake to avoid enemies.

HOW TO BECOME INVISIBLE

As the Shadow Ninja, you can trust me when I say that being invisible is a state of mind. Follow my top tips and I can guarantee you'll leave your enemies blundering in the dark.

TRICK #1
USE YOUR IMAGINATION

When your enemy is being attacked by someone they can't see, they will imagine the scariest foe of all.

Pretend to be the goddess Marishiten, whose multiple arms will terrify anyone.

TRICK #2
PLAN A SURPRISE

If you're planning to wage war on an enemy, don't let them know you're coming. Your enemy will believe you and your entire ninja army magically appeared out of nowhere.

TRICK #3

CREATE A DISTRACTION

If you want to appear invisible during hand-to-hand combat, confuse your opponent with a comment that is so random that they get distracted. Even if they only take their eyes off you for a second, you can convince your enemy that you have disappeared into thin air.

Did I hear you make very nice knitted cushion covers?

Eh?

TRICK #4

MAKE BELIEVE YOU CAN FLY

Make your enemy believe that you have supernatural powers. When you have nowhere left to go, jump up onto a nearby wall or up a tree. Your enemy will either think you've disappeared or that you can fly!

WHATEVER THE OUTCOME, DON'T BE FOOLED INTO THINKING THAT YOU CAN FLY—YOU CAN'T. SO DON'T EVEN TRY.

HOW TO DRESS THE PART OF A NINJA

> I'm an expert in the field of undercover disguises. The black ninja uniform is only one of many different outfits you'll want to master. First, follow these two ninja fashion rules:

ONLY WEAR BLACK AT NIGHT

You probably think ninja wear any color as long as it's black. WRONG. When you need to break into a castle at night or are hiding in the shadows, black IS the perfect color. But if you're out in broad daylight, everyone will see the weird-looking person in black.

NEVER DRESS TO IMPRESS

The most important thing about dressing like a ninja is not to be noticed. Most of the time you just want to look like a normal member of society. Follow my advice and I can guarantee you will never stand out in a crowd.

> Are you a ninja?

> What makes you think that?

DISGUISE #1
THE TRAVELING MONK

Zen Buddhist monks travel constantly, so people won't be suspicious if you're new in town. They also play the flute and wear a basket on their head—what better way to hide your face?!

BASKET HAT
With a basket covering your whole head, you can spy on the crowd without them realizing.

BAMBOO FLUTE
Learn at least one tune to play well, or else you won't be convincing.

NINJA HACK!
Convert your bamboo flute into a poisoned blowpipe called fukiya-zutsu. Roll up a piece of paper and insert it inside the flute to make it airtight. Place a dart, dipped in poison, inside. Ready, aim, fire!

DISGUISE #2
THE PEASANT FARMER

During the Tokugawa period, most people made their living from farming. Acting like a peasant farmer is a great way to learn what everyday people think of their rulers.

STRAW HAT (AMIGASA)

The farmer's hat is designed with a deep brim to keep the sun out of your eyes while working. This makes it great for hiding under!

RAKE (SHINOBI-KUMADE)

This rake is actually a rope threaded through pieces of hollow bamboo. It collapses to become a lethal weapon.

TOWEL (TENUGUI)

Both farmers and ninja are lost without their towel, which has many uses. It can function as a head-covering, a rope, a whip, a sling, or even a towel!

NINJA HACK!

Try this fashion hack to take your peasant disguise to the next level. Cut two eye slits just above the brim of your straw hat. Pull the hat down over your eyes. Now you can watch a crowd while remaining hidden!

DISGUISE #3

THE STREET ENTERTAINER

If you can juggle, perform magic tricks and tell jokes, you could hide in plain sight as a street entertainer. This disguise allows you to be truly outrageous by insulting your enemy in public. Note how people react to what you say—you might pick up some helpful information.

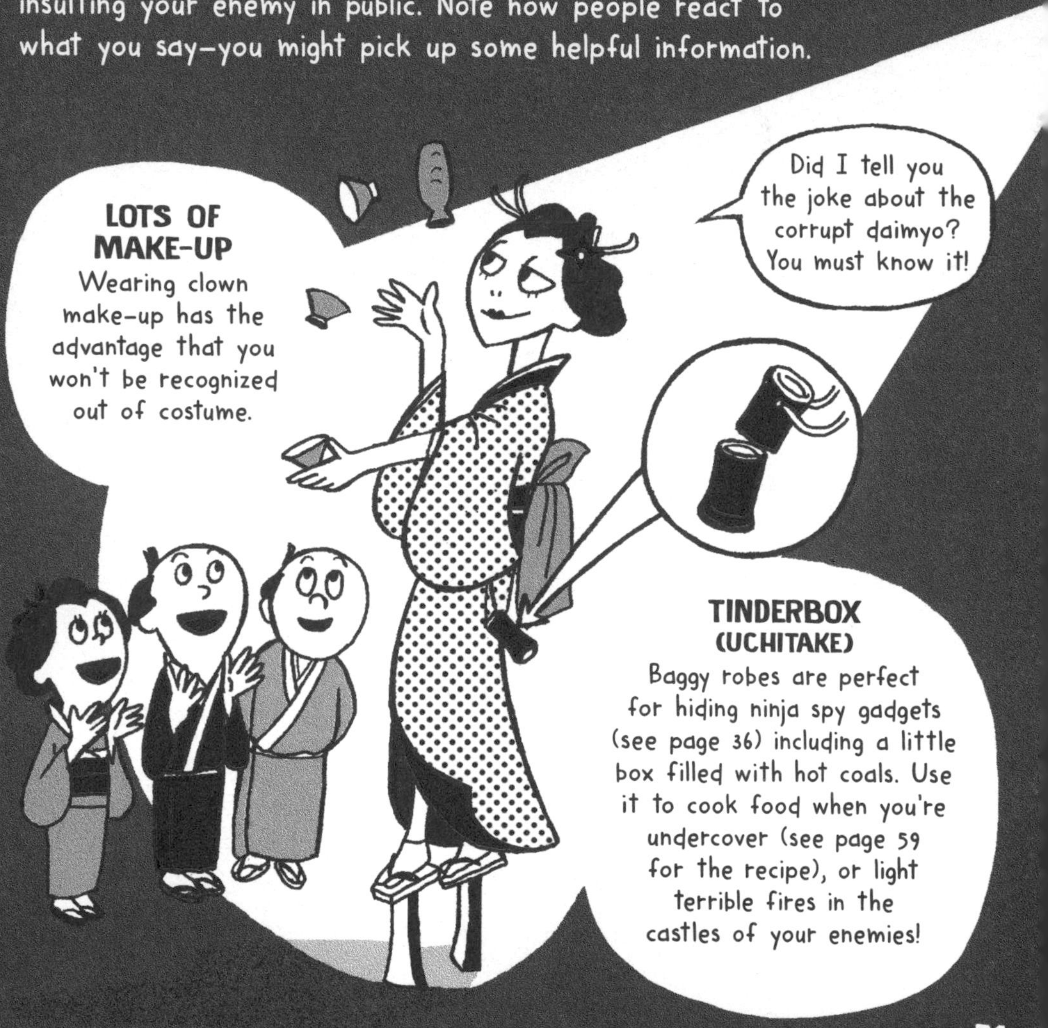

Did I tell you the joke about the corrupt daimyo? You must know it!

LOTS OF MAKE-UP

Wearing clown make-up has the advantage that you won't be recognized out of costume.

TINDERBOX (UCHITAKE)

Baggy robes are perfect for hiding ninja spy gadgets (see page 36) including a little box filled with hot coals. Use it to cook food when you're undercover (see page 59 for the recipe), or light terrible fires in the castles of your enemies!

DISGUISE #4
THE PILGRIM

Iga Province is filled with mountains and temples, so a perfect daytime disguise is to dress like a pilgrim. They beg for alms, or donations, on street corners—the perfect spot for hearing local gossip.

CONCH TRUMPET
Communicate across large distances using a conch-shell trumpet and coded signals.

Psst! Eddie— is that you?

SWORD
As a pilgrim, you can carry around a ceremonial sword without people wondering why.

SANDALS (ZORI)
Basic sandals made from straw, tied to the feet with rope.

NINJA HACK!
Add padding to the soles of your sandals. This will help you to walk, run and jump in silence.

DISGUISE #5
THE COURTIER

If the Shogun fears that his life is in danger from those closest to him, you may need to pose as a member of the Imperial Court to spy on them.

PERFECT PITCH

To blend in, you'll need to speak in a gentle, high-pitched voice and giggle at everyone's jokes— no matter how bad they are.

Eee-hee-hee!! Takeda, you're SO witty!

PERFUME

Apply a delicate perfume and lots of pale make-up to achieve a wilted flower kind of look.

LEARNING THE ROPES

As ninja, our focus is on finding out information, not killing people. Let me show you the ropes that will help you to secure your enemies and keep them tied up.

CATCH YOUR ENEMY

Tied carefully, the Buddha rope, or hotoke-nawa, secures your victim's arms in front of their body. If your aim is to interrogate them, this knot style will allow them to pray to the Buddha for salvation while they leak their secrets to you.

I won't stop tickling until you tell me who you work for!

SCALE A CASTLE WALL

The sageo rope used in combination with a ninja sword (see page 45) is all you need to scale a tall fortress wall. Tie the rope to your sword and use the sword handle as a step up. Pull the sword up after you.

At last, a way to keep Angus out of my room!

KATE'S ROOM

SHUT THE DOOR

Wear a hooked rope, or kaginawa, over your shoulder and around your waist. The hook can be used to wedge a door shut in the face of pursuers when you are breaking into a castle.

35

NINJA SPY GADGETS

You think James Bond has cool gadgets, but where do you think he got all his ideas?! From us ninja, of course!

SECRET DOCUMENT HOLDER (MISSHO-IRE)

Although at first it looks like a dagger for self-defense, the handle is hollowed out so that secret stolen documents can be stored there.

PINE TORCH (MATSU)

Battery-powered flashlights weren't invented until the 20th century. Instead, the ninja carries a wooden torch filled with flammable wax or pine resin. The matsu torch doesn't go out, even in rain, and the tiny tanagokoro-tai matsu torch can be hidden in the palm of your hand.

HAIRPINS
(KANZASHI)

Suitable for women ninja and ninja dressed as geisha, sharp metal hairpins can be stuck into vulnerable parts of the body to weaken your opponent.

PILL CASE
(INRO)

There are many medicines and pills that might be needed on missions —whether to cure yourself, or to poison others. As most people carry pill boxes with them, this item will not look suspicious.

BLINDING POWDER
(DOTON)

If you plan on getting close to your enemy, take some blinding powder with you in an egg-shaped container. Pull the container out quickly and scatter the powder into your enemy's eyes.

KNOW YOUR ENEMIES

The work that you do will be in service of our great lord, the Shogun! Despite the peace he has brought to our lands, there still are those who like to cause trouble...

WANTED!
THE TOZAMA DAIMYO

WANTED FOR: **REBELLION**

DESCRIPTION: The Tozama Daimyo are warlords who tried to overthrow the Shogun. They have since been scattered to the far ends of the country, but they still make trouble!

DEAD OR ALIVE?: They are allowed to live—for now. But keep a close eye on them!

★ REWARD ★
A warm, fuzzy feeling inside!

WANTED!
THE RONIN

WANTED FOR: **ARSON AND VIOLENCE**

DESCRIPTION: The Ronin are samurai who have no master to serve. They wander around the country, and with no battles to join, start fights and cause trouble. They have even been known to set fire to the great Edo Castle, home of the Shogun.

DEAD OR ALIVE?: Dead if necessary, but preferably alive.

★ REWARD ★
Your home and livelihood will remain intact!

WANTED!

THE CHRISTIANS

WANTED FOR: HERESY

DESCRIPTION: Only recently arrived in Japan from Portugal, Christians have a religion that goes against what we Japanese know to be the Will of Heaven. If Christians are allowed to spread their religion in Japan, they will threaten Japanese society! At least they are easy to spot, because they're all Europeans.

DEAD OR ALIVE? Either works for us—they have no souls anyway.

★ **REWARD** ★

Put it this way: you'll be damned if you don't.

WANTED!

THE PEASANTS

WANTED FOR: RIOTING

DESCRIPTION: Despite the wise rule of our great Shogun, sometimes there are revolts in the countryside, and those who work on the land burn crops, kill each other, and generally carry on like a bunch of rascals. Sorry—I mean rioters. This trouble could turn neighbor against neighbor and start a civil war!

DEAD OR ALIVE? Alive!
Just stop them from killing each other!

★ **REWARD** ★
We'll all live to see another day!

WANTED!

THE FOREIGNERS

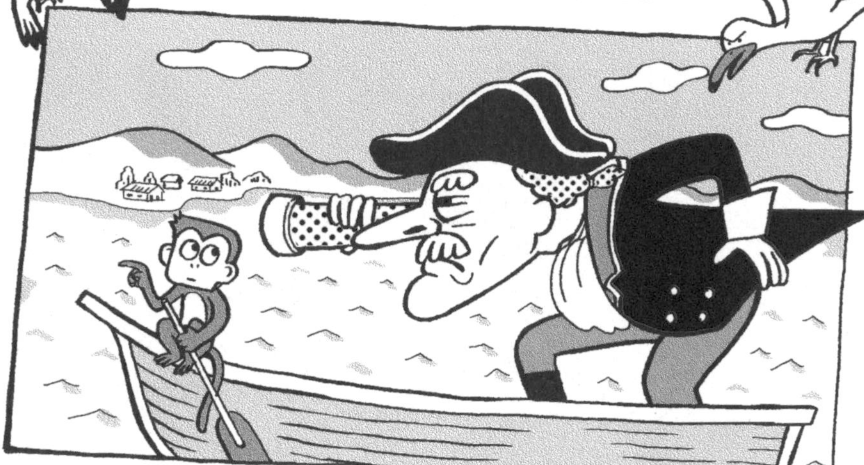

WANTED FOR: **SUSPECTED SECURITY THREAT**

DESCRIPTION: For hundreds of years Japan has been entirely free of foreigners, except for a few Dutchmen and the occasional priest who are allowed to visit. This ensures peace in the land—but the foreigners who are here may be plotting against us! They must be watched!

DEAD OR ALIVE? Alive, please.
Keep a close eye on the scoundrels.

★ **REWARD** ★

Your own peace of mind.

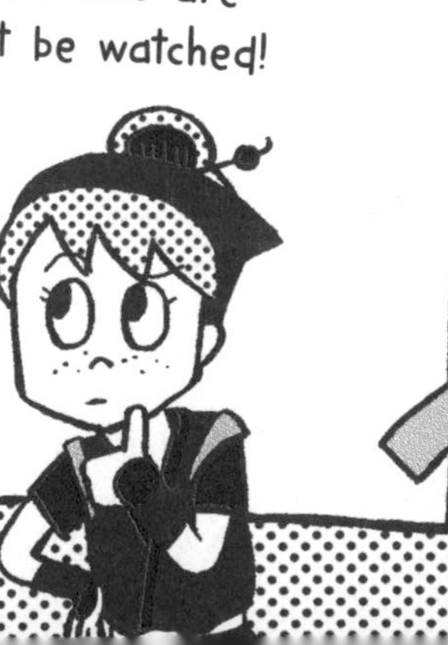

WANTED!
THE CRIMINALS

WANTED FOR: CRIME

DESCRIPTION: Although the land is at peace, there are still secret evil gangs who make money through crime, gambling, threats and murder! Hard to believe! Yet it is true. Unless we stop them now, these crime networks could be here to stay!

DEAD OR ALIVE?
Either/or—as long as they don't kill you first.

★ **REWARD** ★

You should have guessed by now that there are no rewards—this is all part of the job description.

DEFEND YOURSELF

As a ninja, it's your job to escape with your life so you can deliver up-to-date information to your master. Samurai, on the other hand, are taught to fight their enemy to the death. Here's the low-down on the weapons you'll need to defend yourself from samurai:

SAMURAI SWORD

PROS:

✔ elegant and powerful
✔ blade absorbs shock

Yikes! It's not as easy as I thought!

CONS:

✘ your samurai enemy will be more skilled at using it than you are
✘ bulky and hard to carry while climbing
✘ gets caught on clothes and wooden beams

NINJA SWORD

(see page 35)

PROS:

✔ short, straight and easy to climb with

✔ wide hand-guard can be used as a stepping platform when rested against a wall (see page 35)

✔ the sword's strap can be used to tie two swords together (yours and your opponent's)

Wow, this is amazing!

THERE ARE NO CONS!
The ninja sword is specially designed for ninja warriors like you.

45

DAGGER

PROS:

✔ ideal back-up weapon for when you've lost your sword

✔ you can use more than one dagger at once

CONS:

✘ best used at short range—you must get close to your enemy to use it

✘ to pierce your enemy's armor, you need to know its weak spots

I can see the perfect gap!

BOW AND ARROW

PROS:

✔ good for avoiding close-range combat

✔ arrows can be hidden in the lining of a straw hat

CONS:

✘ archers' bows are too big and get in the way of other equipment

✘ can only be used at a distance

NINJA HACK!
Fire arrows can be made using strips of cloth dipped in tar. Tie the strip to the arrow and light it with your tinderbox.

GLAIVE

**PROS:**

✔ cross between a sword and a spear

✔ can be used from a safe distance

✔ can be pointed into the ground and used as a pole-vault to jump over castle walls

CONS:

✘ guardsmen at castles are well-trained to kill with a spear so don't let it get into the wrong hands

YOUR OWN BARE HANDS

Jujutsu is a martial art that trains ninja
to fight hand-to-hand without any weapons.

ONLY PROS:

✔ a great martial artist can seize the
enemy's weapon before they even strike

✔ a jujutsu master can strike from the most
difficult positions, including lying down

✔ your enemy's strength can be used against
them

FLICK

NO CONS!

MUSKET

ONLY CONS:

✘ the lit match needed to set
off a musket, and the flash
and noise when it fires, show
where you are hiding

✘ the force of the explosion can
knock you off your feet

✘ ninja look down on guns as
cowards' weapons

NINJA NEWS
TRUE OR FAKE?

Ninja are such experts at keeping secrets, and have such interesting lives that sometimes the truth is unbelievable. Can you tell the FAKE NEWS from the truth?

HEADLINE #1
NINJA KILL PEOPLE

Ninja (surely the most fiercely trained and disciplined warriors in the world) are masters in the art of assassination, silently killing enemies of the Shogun.

Ninja are most certainly not assassins—this is a nasty lie! Spies, yes, geniuses at escape, yes—but cold-blooded murderers we are not.

R.I.P.
DASTARDLY
DAIMYO

HONORABLE
WARRIOR
KILLED
DISHONORABLY
BY A
GOOD-FOR-NOTHING
NINJA

FAKE NEWS

HEADLINE #2
NINJA ARE MAGICIANS

Ninja can disappear and re-appear at will. They make dragons and serpents appear out of thin air, and create balls of fire and explosions at will, like magicians!

FAKE NEWS

Hee hee! That is just what we want people to think. It is a great compliment that they think so—for it means that our long training has paid off!

HEADLINE #3
THERE'S NO SUCH THING AS NINJA

Ninja don't really exist—they are themselves a myth, made up by the Shogun to scare people!

ONLY SILLY CHILDREN BELIEVE IN NINJA

I know that you know that this last claim is actually false. But for your own safety, you must never admit it. Repeat after me: "There's no such thing as ninja."

TRUE

NINJA - FAKER OR HERO?

Even without social media, liars and playwrights in ancient Japan were very good at spreading stories about famous ninja to confuse and scare the general public. Can you tell the fakers from the heroes?

KATO DANZO

I'm the hero of countless stories and plays. I'm dashing, I can fly, and I'm so powerful, I can swallow a whole bull!

FAKER!
DESPITE HIS POPULARITY, KATO WAS NO MORE THAN A COMMON THIEF WHO STOLE OTHER PEOPLE'S ARMOR.

YAMADA HACHIEMON

I'm a trickster and a master of illusion. I invented a cowl to wear over my head, with two dummy faces fixed to the sides. This makes it look like I have three heads!

HERO!
SURPRISING BUT TRUE! HACHIEMON'S TECHNIQUE IS SO EFFECTIVE, IT HAS BEEN WRITTEN INTO THE SECRET SCROLL OF NINJUTSU TRICKS. TRICKSTERS CAN BE NINJAS TOO!

HATTORI HANZO

I hope you don't think it's arrogant of me to say that I am the greatest ninja of my time. I bravely led the ninja of Edo Castle, and inspired many generations of young men to join our ranks. I am so respected that one of the gates at Edo Castle is named after me.

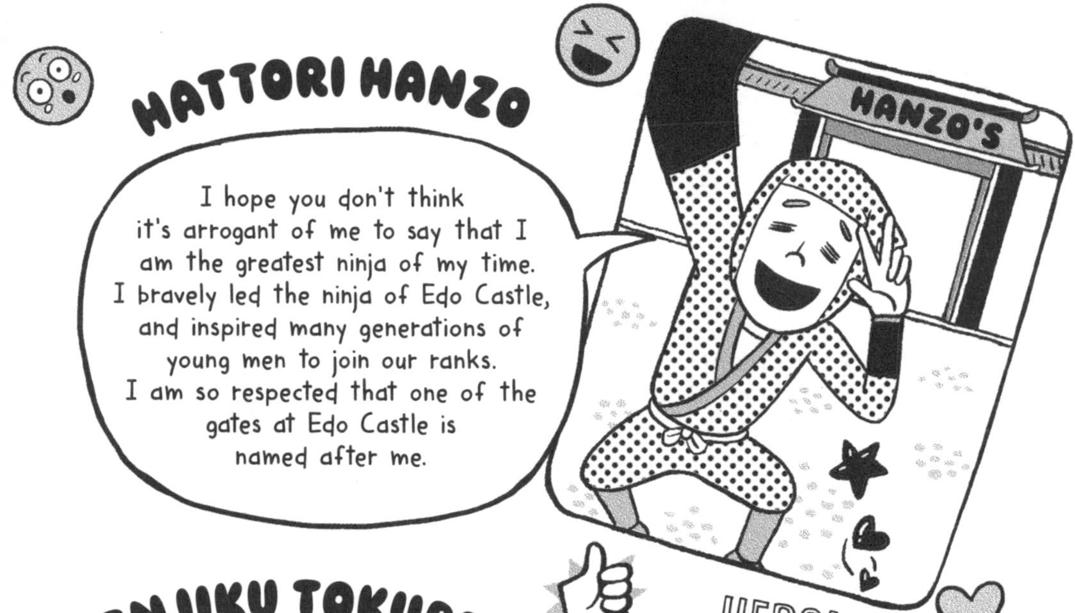
HANZO'S

HERO!
HOORAY FOR HANZO! EVERYTHING HE SAYS IS TRUE!

TENJIKU TOKUBEI

I left Japan to visit India and to improve my wisdom. While I was there I discovered how to turn into a toad!

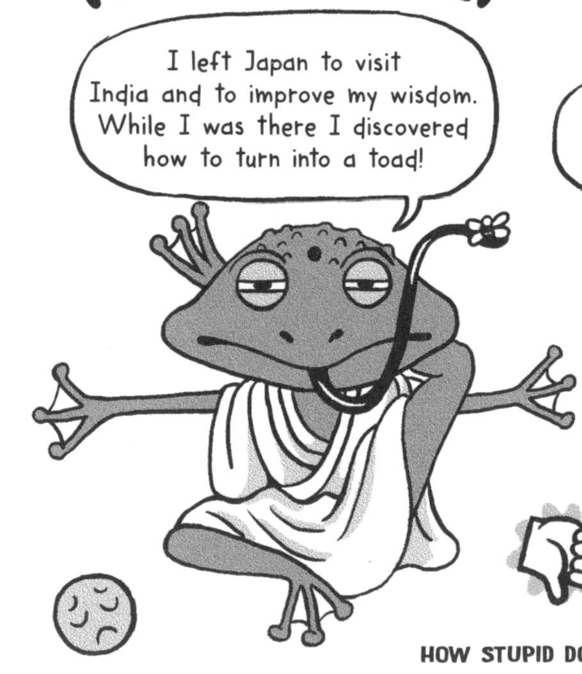

He sort of sounds like Ant-Man, only weirder.

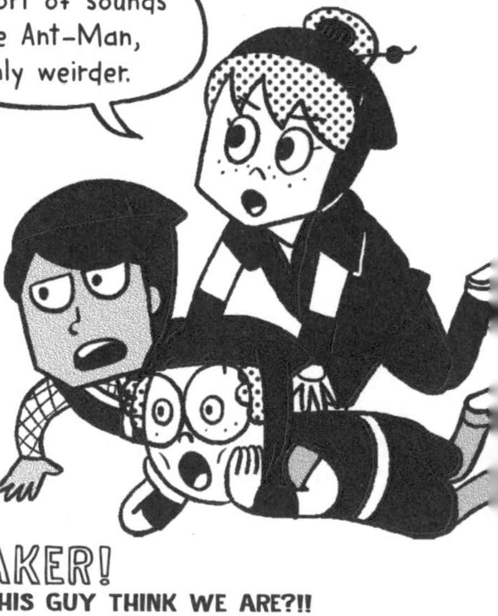

FAKER!
HOW STUPID DOES THIS GUY THINK WE ARE?!!

YAGYU JUBEI

I may look scary, but I am an honorable man. I am from a family of swordsmen who founded the Yagyu Shinkage School of Swordsmanship. It is my honor to serve the Shogun as his personal tutor.

I'm such a big fan!

AUTOGRAPH BOOK

HERO!

THE NINJA WARRIOR JUBEI VANISHED AT THE HEIGHT OF HIS POWERS— FOR TWELVE YEARS (NO DOUBT ON A TOP-SECRET MISSION!). WHATEVER HAPPENED TO HIM, HE RETURNED WITH ONLY ONE EYE. DON'T JUDGE A NINJA BY THEIR APPEARANCE.

NIKKI DANJO

I transformed myself into a rat to steal a scroll. I then used magic to turn myself back into a human!

FAKER!

NINJA ARE BETTER THAN SEWER RATS. HOW DARE HE DISGRACE OUR NOBLE TALENTS?!

MATSUO BASHO

I am the greatest poet in Japan's history. I wrote a poem called "The Narrow Road to the Deep North," which is apparently quite good.

AN ANCIENT POND
A FROG JUMPS INTO
THE SOUND OF WATER

9 10 10

HERO!
BASHO'S HAIKU WAS A MASTERPIECE AND ONE OF THE MOST FAMOUS POEMS EVER WRITTEN.

JIRAIYA

When I'm not riding my giant toad or changing into a snake, I enjoy long walks on the beach with my girlfriend, who is a slug.

Ewww, gross!

FAKER!
UH...THE GIANT TOAD IS A BIT OF A GIVE-AWAY, LET ALONE THE SLUG.

SURVIVAL SKILLS
IN THE WILD

It is nearly time for you to venture out into the real world. It is important that you remember all of these survival skills. Any one of them could save your life!

1. DON'T GET LOST

If you are lost in the wild, my advice is—find yourself again, and quickly. This is where your mega memory for maps will come in handy (see page 23). Pay attention to rivers and waterways. Know the territory in advance!

EDDIE WAS HERE

2. RETRACE YOUR STEPS

If you ARE lost, cut marks into the tree trunks that you walk past, so that at least you can find your way back.

3. USE A COMPASS

Float a needle on a leaf in a puddle of water. It will point north and act as a compass!

4. STARE AT A CAT

During the day you can tell roughly what time it is by looking in a cat's eyes. In the morning they get narrower as the hour gets closer to midday. In the afternoon, they get wider again as the sun goes down. (You may have to check the cat's eyes more than once!)

5. GO WILD

It's possible your mission will require a long journey and an overnight stay in the forest. When you are out in the wild, imitate the other animals that live there. Curl up to sleep like a cat to conserve your warmth and save strength. Sleep on your left side to protect your heart from arrows.

THE NINJA SURVIVAL COOKBOOK

Forget sushi, ramen and shrimp tempura.
These recipes are for when you need to eat
something–anything–to keep you alive...

> Where did I bury my meal?

RICE COOKED IN THE GROUND

Cooking rice without lighting a fire is difficult. The smoke from your fire will show enemies where you are during the day, just as the light from the flames will at night. But the ground beneath the embers of a fire remains hot for a long time after the flames go out. Place a handful of rice in a damp cloth and bury it in the hot ground. Let it slowly cook.

WHEAT-BALL THIRST-QUENCHERS

When water is scarce, make suikatsugan balls by mixing together some pickled plum, wheat flour and sugar. Roll the mixture into palm-sized balls. They're not exactly tasty but they will take away your thirst when you're really desperate (or at least take your mind off it).

THREE-YEAR-OLD LEFTOVERS

Kikatsugan balls will keep you going for hours,
if not days, when there is no other food to eat.
Here's the original recipe:

BLEURGHH!
Maybe I'm not
so hungry.

 INGREDIENTS

Carrots

Buckwheat flour

Wheat flour

Yam

Small piece of liquorice

Cooked rice or barley

Sake (rice wine)

1. Mix ingredients together and soak in sake
(rice wine). Don't worry about the alcohol—
it will evaporate long before you eat it.

2. Knead it all together.

3. Let the dough sit for three years.

4. Serve as balls in emergency situations only.

DON'T TRY THESE AT HOME!
THE STOMACH OF AN ANCIENT NINJA WAS A LOT TOUGHER
THAN YOURS. IN GENERAL, IT'S NEVER A GOOD IDEA
TO EAT SOMETHING THAT HAS BEEN SITTING
IN YOUR POCKET FOR THREE YEARS.

SECRET WEAPONS DEPARTMENT

TOP SECRET

NO BLABBERS ALLOWED

NO UNAUTHORIZED NINJA PAST THIS POINT>>>

If you wish to know more about top-secret ninja weapons, you must first make the following non-disclosure statements:

- ☑ **I PROMISE TO KEEP THESE WEAPONS A SECRET**
- ☑ **I WILL NEVER BREATHE A WORD ABOUT THESE WEAPONS, NOT EVEN IN MY SLEEP**
- ☑ **I WILL NEVER ADMIT TO KNOWING ANYTHING ABOUT THESE WEAPONS, EVEN UNDER TORTURE**
- ☑ **I WILL TAKE ALL SECRETS REVEALED TO ME ABOUT SECRET NINJA WEAPONS TO THE GRAVE**

PROCEED AT YOUR OWN RISK >>>

Ninja weapons are truly deadly and are strictly for self-defense only. Only disciplined ninja can be trusted with them. You can't carry them all at once, so choose the right weapon for the job.

NINJA STARS

These pocket-sized weapons are the perfect way to put off pesky pursuers.

EASY TO USE: ★ ★ ★ ★
Send these steel stars spinning towards your enemy's forehead with a simple flick of the wrist.

DAMAGE: ★ ★ ★ ★ ★
Sharp enough to stun or maim, depending on how accurately you can throw them.

VERDICT: ★ ★ ★ ★ ★
Excellent in an escape situation— which for a ninja is 100% of the time.

ROCKET ARROW

A rocket-powered arrow is a deceptively deadly weapon.

EASY TO USE: ★
Not very. A rocket arrow is heavy and slow to prepare—you need to be strong to use it.

DAMAGE: ★★★★★
Powerful enough to blow up a castle.

VERDICT: ★★
Use on special missions only when complete destruction is required.

THOUSAND-POWER CHAIN

A simple iron chain with a weight at each end doesn't sound too dangerous—until you see how destructive it can be!

EASY TO USE: ★★★
Definitely practice first—it is very easy to knock yourself out with a chain weight.

DAMAGE: ★★★★
The chain becomes 100 times stronger when it is spun and twisted around something.

VERDICT: ★★★★
Ideal for use in an everyday setting where a chain isn't an unusual thing to see.

I thought that was just a bike-lock chain.

63

HAND WEAPONS

WARNING: Ninja hand weapons are not for the faint-hearted.

KNUCKLE-DUSTER

Deliver a knock-out punch by wearing metal knuckle protectors.

RING DAGGER

Spiked iron rings worn on the end of your fingers are good for scratching and gouging during a fistfight.

IRON CLAW

Use sharp iron claws to scratch, scrape, block sword blows or to help climb up the sides of castles.

EASY TO USE: ★ ★ ★ ★
Yes, but you must first get close to your enemy.
DAMAGE: ★ ★ ★ ★
Designed to injure, rather than kill, but they can be deadly if dipped in poison.
VERDICT: ★
Horribly brutal. Only use as a last resort when at risk of certain death.

FIGHTING HOOPS

With sharpened blades both inside and out, these terrible weapons can be used to trap a samurai's sword and turn it away. The other hoop can then be put around your enemy's neck—ouch!

Yikes—these weapons are starting to get gruesome.

EASY TO USE: ★★
These hoops require specialist skills if you want to keep your own fingers intact.

DAMAGE: ★★★★
Simply blunt your enemy's sword or threaten to slice off their head.

VERDICT: ★★★★
For professionals only. These hoops may look innocent, but they can do terrible damage.

NINJA MIND CONTROL

Physical weapons are not your only tools! Work out how to make your enemy do what you want without them even realizing it!

That helmet really does suit you. It brings out the sparkle in your eyes.

1. SHOWER THEM WITH COMPLIMENTS

This shouldn't work so well, but it does. Everyone has their own weaknesses and vanity. Give your enemy presents, tell them how clever they are, and lull them into a false sense of security.

2. TALK BEHIND THEIR BACK

Find out the things that make your opponent angry and upset, and then make sure to talk about them. Your enemy will become unbalanced and full of doubt, and won't act with good judgment. When you have control over them, start planting rumors that help your cause...

I heard the daimyo gets young children to fight for him in battle and that his beard is fake!

3. CAST A DEADLY SPELL

A sneaky way to influence your enemy is to put a curse on them, and let them find out about it. Of course, curses do not work—but they will scare your enemy. For the same reasons, ninja encourage people to think that we are magicians—it makes our enemies worry that they can't fight our powers.

I can't leave the castle or the giant slug will come and force me to marry her!

That reminds me— where IS my poison kit? I put it down earlier, next to that tub of ice cream.

4. OFFER THEM A TREAT

This is much easier—let your enemy swallow a secret mind-control potion you have brewed up with herbs gathered on the mountaintop and mixed with secret ingredients. Mix it in with their favorite food and presto! Your enemy is now open to being controlled.

BREAKING AND ENTERING

I told you that many ninja were criminals in their younger days before joining our order. Thanks to them we have developed useful ways of breaking into castles and slipping out again without getting caught.

STEP 1:
PICK THE LOCK

A true ninja will be able to pick any lock. The coolest lock-picker's tool is the karakuri-kagi. It has different lengths that fold out like a Swiss army knife. Some of them are saws!

STEP 2:
PRY OPEN THE DOOR

The kasugai is a simple U-shaped iron clamp with sharp prongs. Use it to open doors by hammering the sharp prongs into the door and then pulling the clamp like a handle.

It's a sliding door, Angus...

STEP 3:
MAKE A PEEPHOLE
Use a long spike, or kiri, to pierce a hole through a plaster or wooden wall that separates you from your enemy. Now that you have direct access, choose what message you'd like to send them...

STEP 4: LEAVE A MESSAGE

SLEEP WELL
Use the hole to blow poisonous dust into the room for your enemy to breathe in.

PFFFT

SO LONG, SUCKER
Make the hole bigger by scraping out the plaster using a gouger, or kunai. Shoot arrows into the room before making a fast getaway.

YOU'RE COMING WITH ME
Insert the tip of a sharp shikoro saw into the hole and cut through the entire wooden wall panel. If you make the hole human-sized, you will be able to drag your enemy through it and away for questioning.

69

HOW TO WALK SILENTLY

Ninja don't use special ways of walking just to be dramatic. It is important to learn these techniques so your enemy doesn't hear you coming. Choose a walk with a noise level that is right for your mission:

NINJA FOOT WALK

Walk almost on tip-toe. Place your big toe down first. Then slowly lower the rest of your foot.

NOISE LEVEL: the sound of a mouse walking

FLOATING FOOT WALK

Only to be attempted for a few seconds at a time, at critical moments (such as passing the door of a sleeping enemy). It involves moving on the point of your toes and not touching the floor with any other part of your foot.

NOISE LEVEL: the sound of a light breath inward

DOG FOOT WALK

You can walk surprisingly quietly on all fours. And it means you are less obvious to anyone looking around at eye level.

NOISE LEVEL: the sound of a feather falling

FOXY FOOT WALK

Walk like a fox. As in the dog foot, walk on all fours but with only the tips of your toes and fingers touching the ground. It's not easy, but very effective!

NOISE LEVEL: the sound of a snowflake melting

HAND WALK

This the most challenging of all ninja walks! First, crouch into a ball, then walk on your hands. It is completely silent, and allows you to freeze at any moment and pretend to be a rock.

NOISE LEVEL: the sound of silence

71

5 EASY STEPS TO NINJA SUCCESS!

> If you want to fast-track your way to becoming the most successful ninja in the ancient world, follow these easy steps. You'll learn how to spy on the enemy and bring back important information, not to mention find a deep sense of satisfaction.

1. SIZE UP THE ENEMY ARMY

✔ HOW MANY PEOPLE ARE IN IT?
✔ WHAT WEAPONS DO THEY HAVE?

×50

×50

×30

2. KNOW THE LAY OF THE LAND

✔ WHAT STATE ARE THE ROADS IN?
✔ ARE THERE GOOD SPOTS FOR AN AMBUSH?

3. SEE IF THE SOLDIERS ARE HAPPY

✔ DOES THE ARMY LIKE THEIR LEADER?

✔ IS THE MOOD IN CAMP HIGH OR LOW?

✔ HAVE THEY BEEN PAID AND FED RECENTLY?

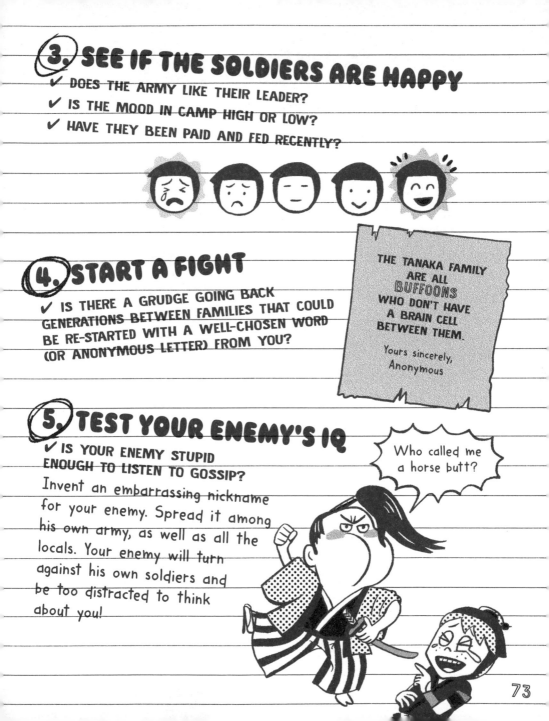

4. START A FIGHT

✔ IS THERE A GRUDGE GOING BACK GENERATIONS BETWEEN FAMILIES THAT COULD BE RE-STARTED WITH A WELL-CHOSEN WORD (OR ANONYMOUS LETTER) FROM YOU?

> THE TANAKA FAMILY ARE ALL BUFFOONS WHO DON'T HAVE A BRAIN CELL BETWEEN THEM.
>
> Yours sincerely,
> Anonymous

5. TEST YOUR ENEMY'S IQ

✔ IS YOUR ENEMY STUPID ENOUGH TO LISTEN TO GOSSIP?

Invent an embarrassing nickname for your enemy. Spread it among his own army, as well as all the locals. Your enemy will turn against his own soldiers and be too distracted to think about you!

Who called me a horse butt?

73

NINJA MESSAGING

HOW TO GET YOUR INFORMATION BACK SAFELY

WRITE A LETTER

Writing a message that is clear in its meaning is harder than it sounds. It's no good if a message travels a hundred miles over craggy mountains only for it to be misunderstood. Specify who or what you are referring to and use accurate times, dates and locations.

> When Angus says "really hairy" do you think he means the enemy or his situation?

TIP
IF YOU ONLY NEED TO SEND YOUR MESSAGE A SHORT DISTANCE, SUCH AS OVER A CASTLE'S WALL, TIE IT TO AN ARROW AND FIRE IT OVER.

SEND A SMOKE SIGNAL

If you want to send your message from a long way away, use a smoke signal. Light a fire on a mountaintop that can be seen for miles. Agree on a code with fellow ninja in advance, for example:

ONE SMOKE COLUMN = ENEMY WEAKENED

TWO SMOKE COLUMNS = ENEMY INJURED

THREE SMOKE COLUMNS = ENEMY DEAD

USE A PASSWORD

If your mission relies on simply confirming or denying a single fact, then you can arrange to use an agreed password with your fellow ninja. Even if you have to meet in a crowded street, no one will know that you are passing on important information.

How was your trip to Edo?

The cherry blossom is particularly beautiful this year.

I have been fishing at my usual place, but they refuse to bite!

Unfortunately I was late for the tea ceremony, and my cup remained empty!

CODE FOR:
IT IS TIME TO ATTACK!
THE ENEMY IS WEAKENED!

CODE FOR:
NOT SURE, NEED MORE
TIME TO COLLECT INFO.

CODE FOR:
OUR INFORMATION WAS
WRONG, THE SHOGUN'S
ENEMY IS NOWHERE TO BE
FOUND IN THESE LANDS.

ATTACK A CASTLE

Fear! Destruction! Panic! They are your friends. When you launch an attack, time is precious. Here are ways to confuse your enemies before they work out what's going on...

BLOCK YOUR ENEMY INSIDE

First locate the army barracks and block the door so the sleeping samurai cannot escape when they are woken. Then open the front gate of the castle so your comrades can enter easily. Set fire to the roofs with burning arrows.

FLAMING BOMBS

If you need to set fire to a castle, you might want a bomb that will burn instead of just exploding. Add wax to the mixture to make it burn for a long time after exploding. Place your bomb into a wicker basket or a clay pot. Light the fuse and run for cover!

SET OFF SOME FIREWORKS

When the Sengokubori Castle was being attacked in 1585, one brilliant ninja archer decided to send a single flaming arrow over the walls and into the gunpowder reserve. The gunpowder exploded, bursting open the castle walls, and ending the battle in a single stroke!

MASTER INFILTRATOR

Kusunoki Masashige was a master at breaking into castles. He was known to set up dummy armies of straw men dressed in armor to terrify his opponents into thinking that his army was huge. He also built a false wall around his fortress that his attackers were forced to climb. It collapsed, killing his enemies.

WATCH OUT FOR
ANTI-NINJA TRAPS

When breaking into a castle, BEWARE of traps that might be in store for you. After all, people are rightly afraid of the ninja!

DANGER! PERIL! GHASTLINESS!

BEWARE

THE HANGING WEIGHT

Samurai will hang a heavy weight from a door frame. It is set off by stumbling over a trip-rope that is almost impossible to see in the dark, causing the weight to fall on your head. It will either knock you unconscious or make you cry out in pain, giving yourself away.

SURVIVAL METHOD:
Look where you are going!

BEWARE THE SPIKED TORCH

Every ninja's nightmare! A patrolling sentry will throw a lit torch out into the darkness to check if anybody is there. If it hits you, it will cause a deadly injury!

SURVIVAL METHOD:
Watch your head and don't make a sound!

BEWARE THE NIGHTINGALE FLOOR

This floor is built in the fortress of Nijo in Kyoto. A foot placed on any wooden floorboard squeaks, making a noise that sounds like birdsong. The lord's bodyguards simply wait for intruders to set off the alarm...

SURVIVAL METHOD: Stay away!

BEWARE THE BLACK HOLE

This simple but effective corridor trap is just a hole in the floor, where several wooden floorboards have been removed.

SURVIVAL METHOD:
Watch out for the gap! Employ the dog or fox foot walk so that you can feel where you are going.

MAKE THE PERFECT GETAWAY

Breaking into a castle is just the beginning.
You now have crucial information that must
be returned to your master. Escaping is all-important!
Here are some clever tricks to help you on your way...

LET THE HORSES LOOSE

Disguise yourself as a samurai so you are able
to wander unchallenged through their army camp.
Find the stables and set all their horses loose
to stampede through the enemy camp,
stirring up chaos and confusion.

> Black Beauty!
> Don't leave me!

DROP BALL SPIKES

As you are running away, drop a handful
of ball spikes, or makibishi, behind you. When
they land, their needles will always point upwards
and get stuck in the feet of your enemies!

THROW NINJA STARS

Sharp metal ninja stars can be thrown in a spinning motion with the flick of a wrist. Nothing is more off-putting to your enemy than to be hit with a ninja star in the forehead!

I can feel a migraine coming on. And right in the middle of a siege.

I hear the gunfire of a thousand snipers —we're doomed!

LIGHT A FIRECRACKER

To strike fear into the hearts of your pursuers, light a firecracker—or better, a whole string of linked firecrackers. The castle guards will think they are being fired at by snipers, even a whole army. Little do they know!

HIDE IN PLAIN SIGHT

If you are at risk of getting caught red-handed and don't have time to escape from the crime scene, use one of these ninja techniques to hide yourself in plain sight.

CREATE A SMOKESCREEN

Cover all trace of your escape by making a smokescreen. Fill a ceramic jar with wolf dung, which is flammable. It will create a smoke that is really black and poisonous to breathe. Set fire to it and throw the jar towards the enemy.

THE QUAIL

Roll up in a ball and pretend to be a rock. Amazingly, this often works in broad daylight!

THE RACCOON DOG

Leap up into a tree just like the tanuki or raccoon dog, and disappear into the branches where the leaves are thickest.

THE FOX

A fox covers his tracks by passing through water to remove the scent and make his tracks vanish. Do the same!

SLIP INTO THE DARKNESS

This is where your black costume can be used to its best advantage. Slip into the darkness and stay there without moving. Chant a silent prayer to the goddess of mercy that you won't be discovered.

LIFE OUTSIDE THE NINJA VILLAGE

Even if you become Japan's top spy, can throw a ninja star with pinpoint accuracy and are honored generously for your service to the Shogun, when you eventually leave the ninja village you will have to pretend that none of it ever happened. Here are some tips on how to blend back into society, or how to avoid society completely:

LEARN SOME CONVERSATION STOPPERS

BECOME A PERSONAL TUTOR

If you reach the top of your career and still feel you have more to give, take inspiration from Yagyu Jubei (see page 54) and become a personal tutor to the Shogun. You will benefit directly from your loyal service and will be well looked after until the end of your days.

That's it! You really have improved a lot since last week, Your Most Illustrious Highness.

I was amazing!

FIND A CAVE IN THE MOUNTAINS

It is said that if you live on a strict diet of kikatsugan (see page 59) you will prolong your life indefinitely. If you make it to 1,000 years old you will officially become a sennin, or old person of the mountains. Enjoy reliving memories of your life as a ninja and live happily ever after in a cave.

THE FINAL DECISION

SO, DO YOU REALLY WANT TO BE A NINJA?

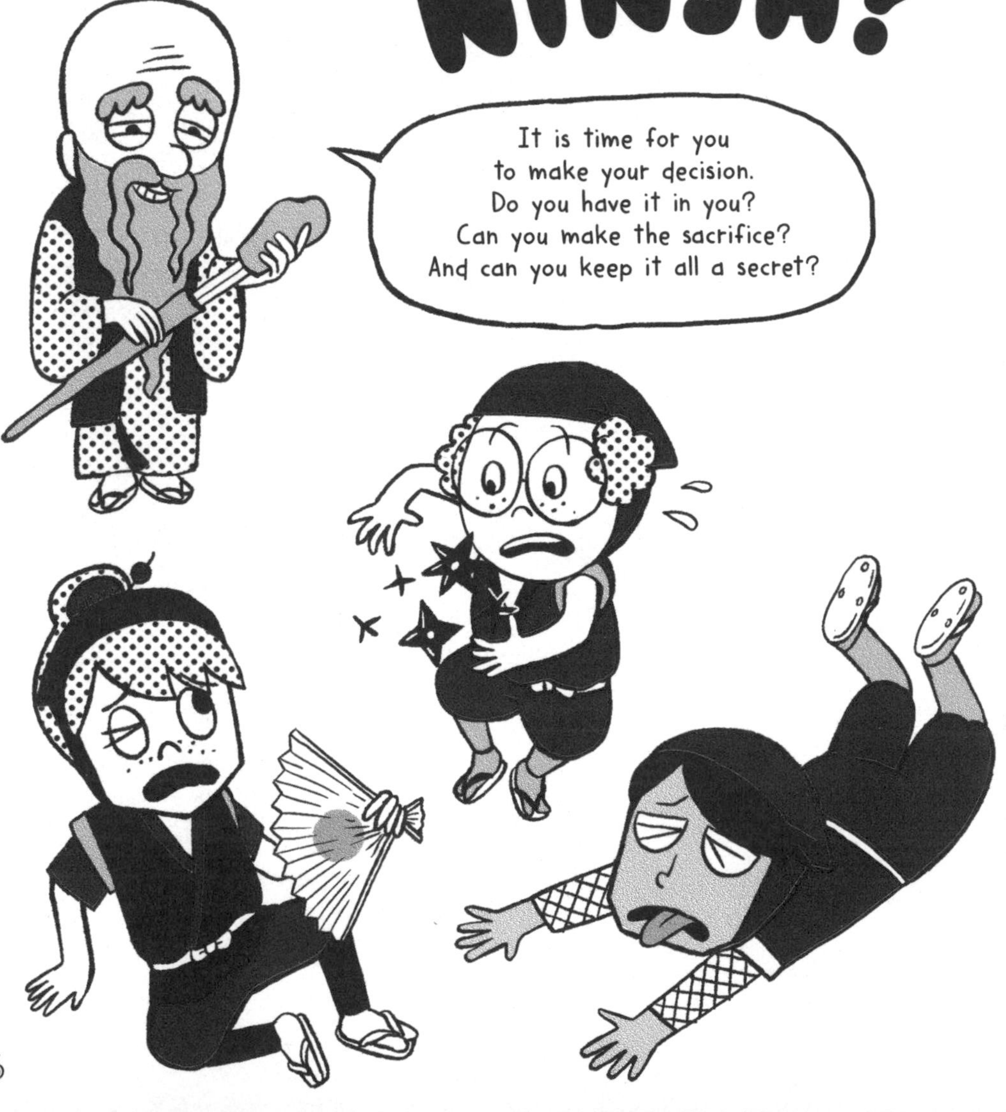
It is time for you to make your decision. Do you have it in you? Can you make the sacrifice? And can you keep it all a secret?

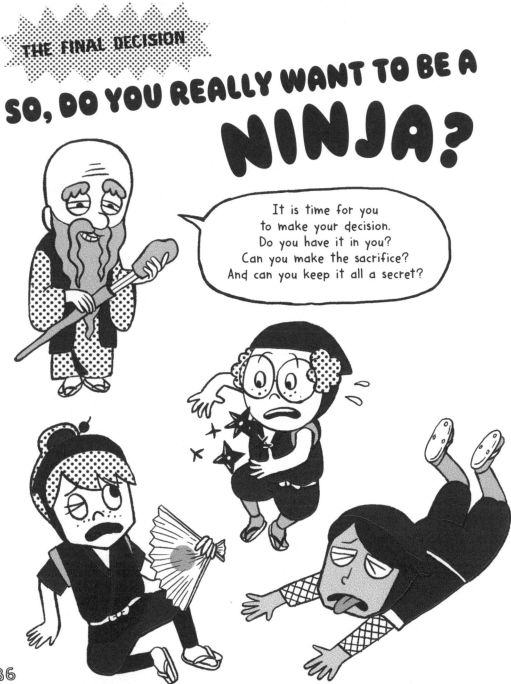

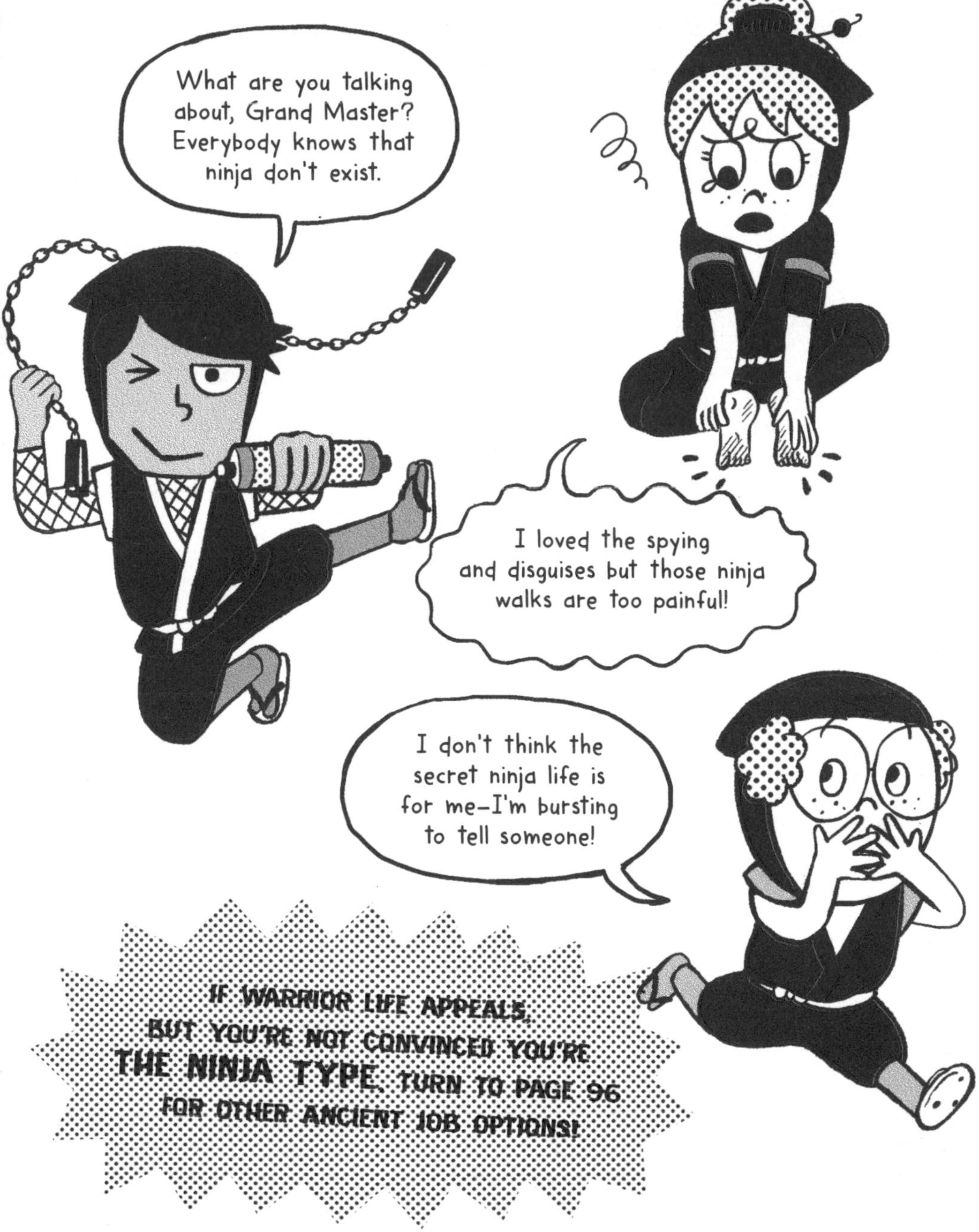
What are you talking about, Grand Master? Everybody knows that ninja don't exist.
I loved the spying and disguises but those ninja walks are too painful!
I don't think the secret ninja life is for me—I'm bursting to tell someone!
IF WARRIOR LIFE APPEALS, BUT YOU'RE NOT CONVINCED YOU'RE THE NINJA TYPE, TURN TO PAGE 96 FOR OTHER ANCIENT JOB OPTIONS!

MAP OF JAPAN

Hokkaido was not part of Japan during the Tokugawa period (1603–1868). The process of uniting the island with the rest of Japan began in 1869.

SCALE
500 km

HOKKAIDO

SAPPORO

SEA OF JAPAN
(EAST SEA)

HOME OF THE NINJA

NORTH

ROAD TO EDO (TOKYO)

LAKE BIWA

KOGA PROVINCE

KYOTO

NARA

IGA PROVINCE

N

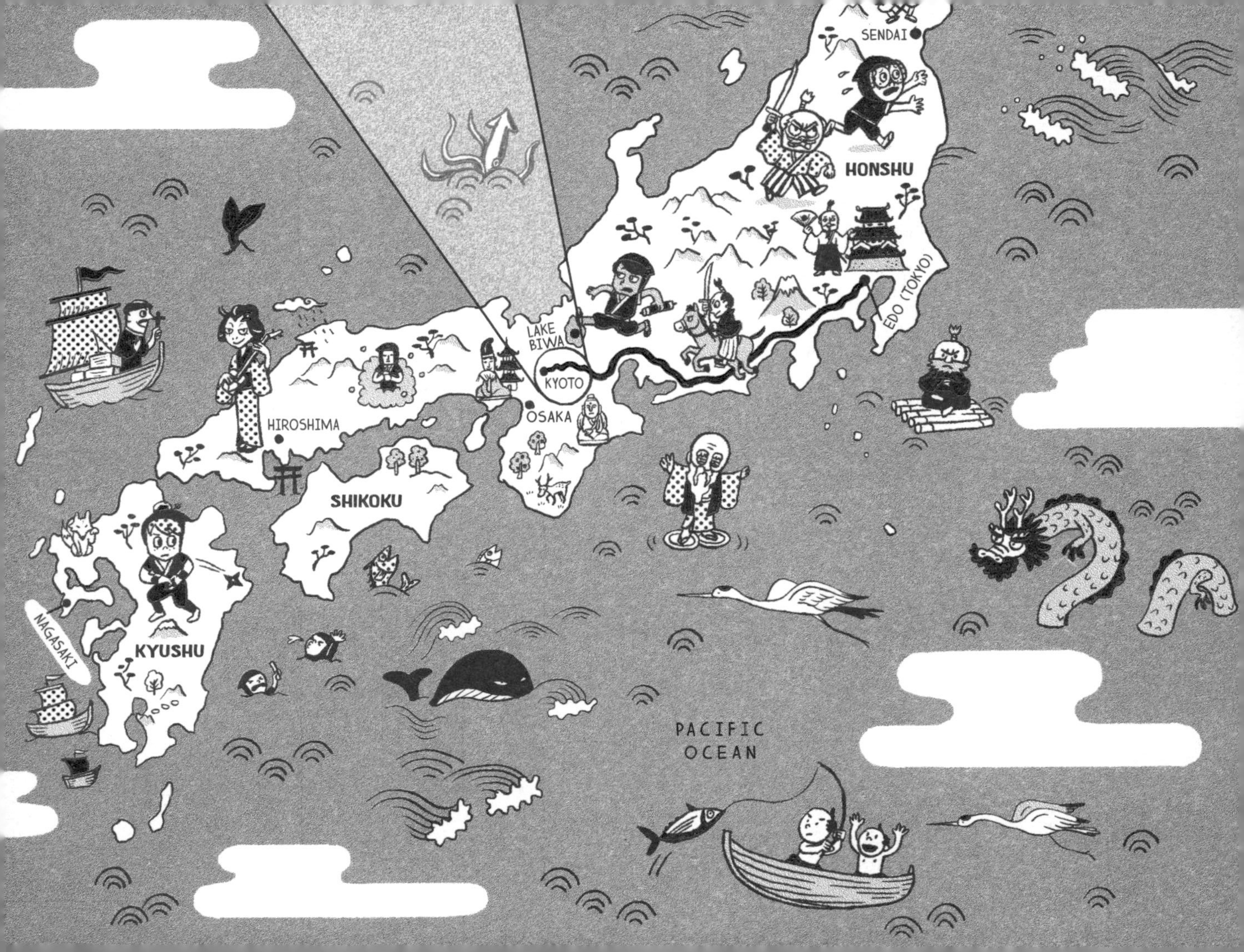
SENDAI
HONSHU
EDO (TOKYO)
LAKE BIWA
KYOTO
OSAKA
HIROSHIMA
SHIKOKU
KYUSHU
NAGASAKI
PACIFIC OCEAN

GLOSSARY

ARCHER a warrior who fights with a bow and arrow

ASHIGARU a foot soldier for the Shogun's Imperial, or royal, Army

ASSASSINATE to kill or murder someone important

BARRACKS the place where soldiers live and sleep

BUDDHA the founder of the Buddhist religion. It is also the name for anyone who reaches a perfect state of enlightenment, or spiritual understanding.

CHRISTIAN a person who believes that Jesus is the son of God

CHUNIN a middle ninja who leads teams of ninja into action and receives the intelligence gathered on missions

CIVIL WAR a war between people living in the same country

COMRADE a fellow warrior or soldier who fights for the same side

COURTIER someone who spends most of their time with the Emperor at the Imperial Court

DAIMYO a warlord who should obey the Shogun but doesn't

FORTRESS a building or group of buildings that are very strong and hard to attack

GEISHA a female artist who entertains others with music, dancing and poetry

GLAIVE a ninja weapon that is a cross between a spear and a sword

HAIKU a type of Japanese poem that is alway written using 17 syllables across three lines. The first line of the poem uses five syllables, the second line uses seven and the third line uses five.

IMPERIAL COURT the center of government and the Emperor's home. In the Tokugawa period, the Imperial Court was at Edo Castle, near Tokyo.

INFILTRATE to secretly break in or intrude on a place

INTELLIGENCE secret information about someone or something

JUJUTSU a martial art focused on hand-to-hand combat

KNUCKLE-DUSTER a metal weapon worn over the knuckles that makes a punch more powerful and damaging

KUNOICHI a female ninja

MARISHITEN the Buddhist goddess of light. Marishiten was worshipped by Japanese warriors who believed she could make them hard to see or invisible.

MIND CONTROL a method for changing the way a person behaves by influencing their thoughts

MONK a man who belongs to a strict religious group. Monks usually live together in a monastery.

NINJA MANSION the house where ninja live and are trained

NINJA STAR a metal weapon shaped like a star for throwing at enemies

NINJUTSU the secret methods used by undercover ninja warriors

OUTLAW a person who has broken the law and has not been caught

PEASANT a poor farm laborer who may or may not own land

PILGRIM a person who travels to a sacred place for religious reasons

RONIN a samurai who has become unemployed because their master has died or lost all their wealth

SAMURAI an upper-class warrior trained to protect the Emperor

SENNIN an old person who lives in the mountains

SHOGUN the military ruler of Japan. During the Tokugawa Period the Shogun was Tokugawa Ienari. He employed ninja to protect him from his enemies.

TINDERBOX a box holding either materials or an object that can be used to light a fire

TOKUGAWA PERIOD a peaceful time in Japan between 1603 and 1868

WARLORD a military leader with control over an area of land

ZEN BUDDHISM a school of Buddhism that believes self-control and meditation can help people to understand the world

So YOU'RE the Shadow Ninja!

NINJA HAND SIGNS

These top-secret hand signs called "kuji in" can help you to hypnotize your enemy and will give you a supernatural boost in power. At the same time as you say the sound related to each sign, cut the air with your arm, as if with a sword. This will construct an invisible barrier of protection between you and your enemy.

THE HAND SIGN

THE SOUND

rin   pyo   to

sha   kai   jin

retsu   zai   zen

INDEX

If you want to be an ancient warrior, you'd better become a **VIKING** or a **ROMAN SOLDIER**. After all, **NINJA** don't exist.